Ecstasy

The World of
SUFI POETRY
and PRAYERS

Nahid Angha, Ph. D.

International Association of Sufism Publications

The International Association of Sufism is a publisher of
many Sufi books and Sufi related materials. Books/articles
published by the IAS are the authors' views and the Publisher
takes no responsibility for any statement made by the authors
in its publications.

Cover design: Soraya Chase Clow
Photograph: Murshida Batul Martha Burk

Acknowledgment:
Special thanks to Roger Olmsted for his editing of the
manuscript.

For more information address the publisher:
International Association of Sufism
PO Box 2382
San Rafael, California 94912
USA

Printed in the United States of America

Table of Contents:

Praise be to Allah, Most Gracious, Most Merciful, the Compassionate; the Beginning and the End, the Apparent and the Hidden, who has created human being in the best of form, and Love as the essence of all creation, and entrusted this splendid essence into the heart of the chosen human being.

Praise be to Allah, the Aware, the Just, the All Knowing, who has illuminated the hearts of His servants by His light, and opened their eyes to the beauty of enraptured love.

Asalamu salat ala siyedena Mohammad, salute to the Messenger of Allah: Mohammad, *habib Allah,* a mercy for the creation, a standard for humanity, whose immeasurable devotion and love for Allah has taught the Sufis the art of submission to the Divine. It is from his teachings that the spring of Sufism flows, and the glory of Sufis surpasses the test of time.

Praise be to *Moulay-e-Motaghian*: Amir al Momenin Ali from whose generation Sufism has been glorified. And glory be to the Sufis, the mystics of Islam, the religion of submission to the Will of Allah, for they have inspired humanity to search for eternal essence of love in the solitude of the heart.

Introduction

Some time ago, following the publication of *Selections: Poems from Khayam, Hafiz, Rumi, and Moulana Shah Maghsoud* (1991), and *Sufism: The Journey of The Lovers* (1998), and the celebration of Sufi poetry and music at the Annual Sufism Symposia of the International Association of Sufism (1997 & 1998), many of my fellow travelers–spiritual sisters and brothers–asked me to write and translate more selections dedicated to Sufi poetry and prayers. By that time, *Selections* had been sold out; only a short chapter in *The Journey of the Lovers* was dedicated to Sufi poetry. Because of these requests, a result of sharing some of the writings and poetry in my previous works, I thought it was timely to write and translate this book on Sufi poetry and prayers.

Within the covers of this book we will venture to the shore of the ocean of Sufi poetry and prayers, and enter into the magnificent world of rapture and glory that these poems unlock. And yet our stay shall be brief: this is only a sample of the sweet fragrance of the Sufis love poems and prayers for Allah, the Truth, the All Embracing. Yet, though brief, it comes from the pure heart, as does all truth. Here, we will read from the book of the hearts of Sufi poets.

Sufis are the gnostics of Islam; they are the seekers of the hidden essence of knowledge. Their study of Qur'an and the teachings of the Prophet is necessarily very deep, so much so that it is expressed best in the allusive symbolism of poetry–the most difficult, most ancient, and most pure form of writing. Sufis do not write dry commentaries on the sacred text, works which convey only information and limitation. Neither do they entrust their understanding of the sacred text to the hand of chance imagination or speculation. Poetry and prayer avoid both of these linguistic and mental traps. Because Sufis witness what they learn, and see what they know, they break the limitations of the ordinary and the dimensions of time and space in their understanding. To express this higher understanding, only the highest form of expression of language is suitable.

Sufis know that each word of the sacred book of Qur'an reveals a unique and distinct meaning that is accessible, not through the mere common definition of words, but through the understanding of their essence. Because of this, each of these meanings opens a door towards understanding the essence of Being. It is from such longing for the truth of Being that the pillars of Sufism have remained strong over the centuries, even as the shifting colors of the apparent world have changed in their bewildering multiplicity.

The Prophet taught us that the pursuit of knowledge is the duty of every Muslim. In all he did, the Prophet battled the darkness of ignorance, and Muslims must continue this struggle, away from darkness and towards the light of pure illumination. Sufis have acknowledged, through their submission to Allah, that the pursuit of knowledge in general, and especially the inner knowledge of understanding the Divine, is their particular duty. For more than a millennium, Sufis have made a gift of this knowledge to the world, and so have contributed magnificently to civilization and its progress. Their contribution ranges from science to literature, from the beauty of architecture to the refinement of astronomy and many great advances in mathematics, from medicine to philosophy and ethics. These achievements represent not only the outward form of knowledge, but also manifestations inspired by inward understanding.

Sufi poets bring an extraordinary contribution to both the world of religion and the world of literature. To many, these worlds may seem very different—the one, universal, the other, highly personal. Yet in their love poems for Allah these two worlds come together in the unity of Divine love. The beauty of their words and the system of mutually referential symbols that form their imagery create a language of understanding that both expresses and explains the principle of Sufism, a state of Divine rapture and ecstasy, into to the heart of their listeners. They speak of the beauty of annihilation of one's self into the Will of Being; they write of the transience of the world of superficial existence; of the grace of nature; of the longing of the lover; of the dignity of the human heart. Their words speak to us as messengers of the soul, of the Divine, Allah, that embraces all life. They speak to us through their humanity to our humanity in its truest meaning. The message of Sufism is always hidden behind the surface of their words in the special system of symbolism that generations of Sufi poets have developed to express their understanding in melodies, songs, and music, in their sonnets and masnavi, quatrains and prayers.

Because of this, Persian Sufi poetry as well as others is tremendously difficult to translate into English. Many of the translations commonly available are the works of English Orientalists of the 19th and early 20th century, who had only little knowledge of the primacy of the system of symbols that unify Sufi poetry, and, worse still, often wrote their English translations in strict rhyming couplets, the most conventional and restrictive form of English verse. The meter and rhyme structure of Farsi verse are completely different from the English rhyming couplet. As a result, their works, presented and widely sold today as translations, are in fact something quite different—conventional Victorian English poetry more or less loosely based on Sufi texts, expressing English ideas of what Sufi poetry would be like if it were written by romantic Englishmen. These translations have a place in English verse, but they do not accurately represent the meaning intended by the Sufi poets.

While reading Sufi poetry, it is important to remember that while the English language naturally is structured around gender pronouns, Farsi is not structured in this way. In the translation of Sufi poetry the usage of gender pronouns is therefore often unavoidable. Therefore, in Farsi, the words Beloved and the Lover, which are central to Sufi poetry as symbols for the Divine and the human, are free from the limitations and many implications of gender differences. However, since these Sufi poets were men, the Beloved is most often portrayed as a woman. In this, Sufi poets break radically from the traditions of the many religions, such as Christianity, in which God is explicitly male. This reversal of conventions so familiar in the West is more a special form of poetic expression; certainly, these Sufi poets did not conceive of the Supreme Being as either male or female. Rather, since the usage of female imagery cannot sensibly be taken literally, it serves as a striking example of the symbolism of Sufi's poetry, in which each term used represents a mystical meaning. When we have occasionally used "He" in these English translations referring to God, Divine, Allah, we do so only to follow the rule in English that uses the masculine pronoun in a general sense that does not necessarily imply the male gender (e.g., "mankind"), whereas the use of the female pronoun traditionally always implies the female gender, and the neuter "it" is used in English to refer to things, never to intelligent beings. For Sufis, God is not identified with either gender, and is certainly not a neutered thing.

As a Persian Sufi, from the old school, who has well traveled the path of Sufism and is aware of its stations and stages, it is my duty to offer a few words of caution. I have undertaken these translations with the realization that much is necessarily lost, since how can one translate the universe of a heritage, a culture, a language, a way of life, a sacredness of a religious belief, a history, known metaphors, and people who embraced such treasures, into a new universe of different characteristics? I have chosen to give primacy to the sense of the poems, especially the complex system of metaphors that bind it together. These metaphors cannot be understood through any one poem standing alone; but the reader can gain some sense of this symbolism by seeing metaphors appearing in different contexts in different poems.

Let us review an example of the use of the Sufi system of symbolism by comparing a few Sufi poems. Here is one from Hafiz's sonnets. He writes:

On the tablet of my heart
There is nothing engraved
Except the alif like figure of the Beloved.

One can write books on any one of these metaphors: tablet, heart, alif, the Beloved, the alif like stature/figure, for each one carries an old history, expressing the depth of Hafiz's personal knowledge, his religious belief, and above all references to the sacred book of Qur'an, all written in a complex symbolic language of Sufism.

For example, "alif" is not simply a letter in the alphabet of Arabic or Farsi languages. "Alif", unity of the Divine, reflects the annihilation of the traveler into the essence of Being; the strength of one's belief; holding the steadfast rope (referring to a verse of Qur'an), and more. For Sufis, it serves as just one of many instances of meaning unwrapped within meaning.

The difficulty does not stop at this point. One must be cautious of the knowledge of the translator, most often, portrayed in the translation; and, his loyalty to the poet's meaning or, most commonly, his understanding of it. For example, I have seen the following verse, from Rumi's *Diwan-e-Shams-e-Tabriz,* translated and used to support a different meaning, perhaps the intention or understanding of the translator rather than what Rumi (Moulana Jallaleddin Moulavi, known as Rumi, 13th century Persian Sufi) intended to relate:

> *A testimony, a declaration, Oh, Muslims!*
> *I know not myself.*
> *I am neither a Christian, nor a Jew,*
> *A Zoroastrian, or a Muslim.*

A translator or reader may take this testimony literally, and conclude that Rumi did not belong to any religious system. However, if we continue and do not ignore and overlook a few verses down the page, we see a different intention and message:

> *Duality was removed, I see only a Unity*
> *I search, I confess, I know*
> *And call upon the Only One.*
> *You are the Beginning, You are the End;*
> *You are the Apparent, You are the Hidden;*
> *I know nothing other than*
> *Hu and Ya Manhu.*

In these verses, as in all his poems, Rumi refers to the verses of the sacred book of Qur'an, reflecting the holy verses of: *la ilaha illa Allah*, there is nothing except the One, Allah; Allah is the Beginning, and the End, the Apparent and the Hidden, and all knowledgeable (direct quotation from the Holy Qur'an). And "You" refers to Allah, and "Hu" refers to Allah, the Almighty. In other words, Rumi's expression of his state of annihilation in Allah, where all there is, is but Allah; certainly reflects a Muslim's confession.

As we see in Sufi poetry, words and systems of phrases are never used lightly, and are never used in isolation. Instead, the poem as a whole resembles a tightly-bound package, a treasure box for the reader to unpack or a joyful puzzle for the reader to solve, and in its unpacking through careful reflection, one attains insights of understanding. For the listener, the poem sings a melody with its own musical language for the listener to decipher. Sufi poems and prayers have a language of their own, very much different from any spoken, everyday language. Sufi poets always refer, though often in complex allusions, to the verses of Qur'an and the teachings of the Prophet in their poetry. If the reader is not familiar with these teachings, and cannot understand and grasp the allusions, then the poem truly becomes an indecipherable code and one's interpretation remains inadequate in understanding the depths that lie veiled behind the magnificent words of the Sufi poet. This inadequacy is seen even more if the translator is born and raised in a different culture than that of the Sufi and in a religion other than Islam.

Sufism has a structure of its own.

Sufi poets are masters of sonnets and quatrains, structures of verse that, in their meter and complex patterns of rhythm, cannot be directly translated into other languages. In these following translations, the original meaning of the poet as it is expressed through the rich system of symbolism of Sufi metaphor, has been adhered to as closely as possible.

The universe of love demands glory and richness, and Sufi poets are rightfully regarded as meriting an unsurpassed place among the world's poets in creating such glorification of love.

While their metaphors paint the colors of the flower fields, and their rhythms and rhymes create the melodies of the nightingales and songs of nature onto the pages of a book, yet there exists a deep meaning behind each word and rhythm to be sought and found.

> *Neither cold nor hot this fine breeze blows*
> *The dust cloud from the rose garden of desire.*
> *Nightingale singing "Drink! Drink your Wine!"*
> *To the loving heart of the yellow rose.*

Hakim Omar Khayam
(11th century Persian Sufi)

The portrait of the Sufi's Beloved is so magnificent that one falls in love with the beauty of that Beloved, a Beloved hidden within and behind the world of nature. Sufi poets constantly create magnificent works of ecstasy in their glorification of the Divine message. Their poetry becomes a manifestation of the Beloved, Allah; and the poet is not just mere clay, or dust returning to dust, but rather illumination of the light of the heart breathed into the heart of nature. "....When I fashioned him,

I breathed into him from My spirit...." Qur'an
(15:29) (32, 9)

> *I am life from the Beloved*
> *Not mere clay but rather*
> *The light of heart*
> *Breathed into the heart of dust.*
> *I am the soul of the spirit,*
> *And so my heart resides beyond the spheres,*
> *For my life springs forth from His commanding,*
> *Earth from heaven, life hidden in dust.*

Moulana Shah Maghsoud
(20th century Persian Sufi)

The Sufi discovers unity in this rapturous state of love and melts away into the being of the Beloved, where there remains no separation, nothing of the lover: all that remains is the Beloved, for there is nothing other than the Beloved, the Truth: *la illaha illa Allah.*

And he declares:

> *I wonder at this You and I,*
> *You are all there is*
> *And I am all annihilated,*
> *And I exist no longer.*

Mansur al-Halaj
(10th century Persian Sufi, who was executive
for proclaiming: I am the Truth.)

We searched awhile for the Divine
Within the depth of our illusions
Looking there to find His signs
In the beings of "You" and "I".
When love appeared
"You" and "I" were dissolved
No more need to follow signs.

Moulana Shah Maghsoud

The heart longs for the Beloved, weeping tears of separation, tears as abundant as the stars that fill the heavens. The Sufi expresses this longing in poetry, and one of the poets who brings such longing to hearts is Moulana Jallaleddin, Rumi, who begins his magnificent *Masnawi* with the longing of the reed:

Listen to the singing of the reed
To melodies of plaintive separation:
A listener I need,
One with a longing heart
To whom I shall sing my songs.
Reed sings to you the story pure
Of lovers and Beloved
Of longing hearts that have endured.
Beloved, You alone remain,
And so it matters not
If my life is passing away.

or

Oh, lovers: let deception depart,
Come and join the drunkard.
Rise from the heart of fire
To become a butterfly,
One foot upon your ego, the other on the world,
Then and only then
May you seek refuge in the house of the drunkard.
Purify your heart, cleanse your soul,
Leave your jealousy, ill will and all:
Then and only then become a Cup
For the Wine of Love.
Turn into life deserving of the Beloved
If you would journey towards the house of the Wine
Bearer: Come Drunkard.

The story of my rapturous love
Brings fantasy to your thoughts.
Friend, become annihilated
As an eternal lover,
Become ruin and naught:
Then, and only then
Your story becomes a sweet legend,
A fantasy, a dreamlike love.

One's heart finds union with the longing of the
Sufi poet; after all, is there anyone who has not

experienced the bittersweet taste of love?

A field of flowers,
A Cup of Wine,
And the Beloved by my side.
With such wealth
The king is my servant tonight.

Khajeh Shamseddin Hafiz Shirazi
(13th century Persian Sufi)

Sufi poets use many symbols to speak of the Eternal Unity. Metaphors such as "Wine," "Cup," "Wine Bearer," "Drunkard" or "Drunken," "ruins," "annihilation," or "tulip" are most often used in Sufi poetry or prayers to express Divine love and the state of unification. In Sufi prayers and poetry, "Cup," (*jaam*) refers to the heart that holds the Divine Wine; while "Wine" (*sharab*) serves as a unifying symbol for love (*Ishq*). These words express the extremity of Divine love, a longing for unification, where the lover is saturated by love for the Beloved. From the apparently paradoxical idea of wine a symbol is created: for the Sufi does not drink wine, as wine drinking is forbidden in Islam. The paradox is, characteristically, resolved on a higher level by a reference to the Qur'an: "... And their Lord will give them a drink of Wine, Pure and Holy." (76:21, *Al-Insan*) Thus, the Sufi poet uses wine to refer to *sharaban tahura*, the pure wine, referring to this verse of Qur'an. In all Sufi poetry and prayers, the Sufi becomes drunk from this pure wine. The Divine, the eternal Beloved of all, is expressed by the figure of the wine bearer, who offers this wine and pours into the cup (the heart), of those who are fit to receive it.

> *A vessel of Wine, a book of Love*
> *A loaf of bread to pass the time,*
> *And You and I are in the ruins,*
> *A feast beyond the dream of a king*

Omar Khayam

Sufis have stepped beyond the limits of time and the confines of mind to take the journey of the heart towards the Eternal, where the heart must be sacrificed at the doorstep of the Friend. All these words and metaphors point to the subject of love as the rule of attraction, the key to survival through annihilation into the Divine, into Being.

All of this makes for a complex system of metaphors, bound together in verse, that is at times difficult to translate into English without explanation. For example, drunkenness, intoxication, drunkard and ruins, may have a negative sense in English because these terms might be taken literally; quite the opposite of the often paradoxical symbolism deliberately used in Sufi poems to express, through a system of hidden signs that demand understanding, the essence of truth that cannot be expressed in the direct language of prose. Intoxication and drunkenness refer to being saturated by Divine love, and "ruins" is the heart of a lover, a heart saturated by this love. This is one of the ways in which Sufi poetry presents a puzzle to the reader: how can such gloomy words be used to express ecstasy? As I have suggested, an important reason lies in the understanding of language as a puzzle, a system of signs that must be deciphered in order to be understood. Yet once one recognized these terms and their meanings, a whole new world of beauty begins to open and a new understanding unfolds.

The acceptance of paradox highlights the fact that language is an imperfect system of signs that can mislead as well as tell truths; apparent paradox expresses the understanding that essential truths are to be found hidden beneath apparent meanings. Words serve as a manifestation of truth, just as nature expresses Being in a world of the manifestation of beauty. In the words of the Sufi poets, just as in the world of nature, every manifestation brings riches into existence; every movement is a longing for a beloved, and all are participants in the dance of love. Just as the moth (which in Sufi poetry is called "butterfly" instead of "moth") circles ever closer to the flame of the candle, and the blackened heart of the tulip is burnt with the fire of love, the Sufi drenches the robe of piety with wine and calls upon us to leave the superficial world of reason, of insinuation, of illusion, of calculation, of question, of deception, behind.

In their teachings, Sufis direct one to treasure the present moment of life and celebrate each breath with great admiration for life. They speak in the knowledge that time is passing; the fact that their work remains relevant throughout the centuries makes this realization all the more poignant.

The rose's song rang out amidst the garden:
Leaves of fine gold, one upon another;
Smiling laughter, too,
I brought into this world of colors.
Then from all this,
My blossom bursting, scattered
I gave my petals to this world
*   Where nothing matters.*

Omar Khayam

The themes of love and the Divine form the foundation for great poetry precisely because it is here that humanity is brought into confrontation with the essential. Sufi poets speak the universal language of love, of its longing nights and dream-like days.

The Sufi longs for unity with the incomparable Beloved, and on this journey, his heart finds its way to the doorstep of the Beloved, where nothing else matters.

Oh, Allah, I cannot liken You to any,
For You are beyond comparing.
My words cannot describe You,
For You alone describe Yourself.

Khajeh Abdullah Ansari
(11th century Persian Sufi)

Sufis, free from the confines of time and place, use this magnificent language of love with the utmost grace and perfection. These masters of exceptional experience of Divine unity bring their delight, a bittersweet recognition, to the heart of their listeners.

Sufism is faith in its perfection, belief saturated by the fragrance of the Divine.

Yet this is not the path of sleepwalkers or restful dreamers, but the path of illuminated, enlightened hearts:

Your hair is tangled,
Tossed by midnight breeze,

Your smile enraptures
A melody sung:
A cup of wine.
    Your eyes half closed with sleep,
    Your lips delightful,
    You came to my night and whispered:
    Oh, eternal lover,
    Are you sleep tonight?

Hafiz

On the journey of the heart, we each walk our path alone, and worship the Divine in the solitude and privacy of our hearts. The great world of ecstasy is hidden within the nature of humankind. "Do not think of yourself as a small body" said Amir al Momenin Ali (7th century Arabia) to whom almost all schools of Sufism are related, "as a greater universe is wrapped within you."

The Divine breath, eternal music,
Found its way to the Sufi's heart.
A song is heard, a song is heard:
You are the Truth,
You are beyond all measure.
    Your beauty saturates my heart
    Its fragrant sweet and delightful.
    Take my mind, an offering, a gift
    You are the Truth,

You are beyond all measure.
The Cup, the Wine, and the Vessel
The eternal beauty
Are fragrance of Your Being:
You are the Truth,
You are beyond all measure.

Being is Yours
Eternally Your name
I am submitted to Your will
You are the Truth,
You are beyond all measure.

Moulana Shah Maghsoud

Let me end this introduction with a poem from the Master of the Pure Ones, the *Wali*, the Guide, *Moulay-e-Mutaghian*, Amir al Momenin Ali (7th Century, Arabia)– a poem reflecting the universe of a Sufi:

Oh, Allah: All Praises belong to You.
You are the Generous, You are the Merciful,
You are all Knowing, All Seeing, All Hearing.
You know my poverty, You know my obedience,
You hear my silent praises and whispers,
Every moment of my life.

All praises are due to Allah.
Nahid Angha

Khajeh Abdullah Ansari, known as Pir-e-Harat, was a prominent Sufi master of eleventh century, Persia. His famous prayers: The Munajat, is considered one of the most profound expressions and prayers in Sufism. Followings are a few of his prayers from his Manazel-al-Saerin.

Oh, Allah,
I call upon You;
You open the hearts towards prayer
You bring love and devotion in the solitude
   of Your servants.
You glorify the breath of those who keep
   Your secrets.
My only friend is Your remembrance
My only thought is to honor Your presence
My only guide towards You is You.
I address You, the Divine;
You are the rememberer and the
   remembered,
You are the reason of all being
Only You deserve to remember Yourself
Who deserves such grandeur except You?

Oh, Allah, the All Knowing,
No words can praise You
     except those of Your own.
No one can treasure
Your blessings but You.
Nothing can heal the longing
     for Your presence
          except Your sweet fragrance.
Show me the way towards Your presence, as
     my praises fall beneath Your footsteps.
My mind is limited to recognize Your beauty,
     and my body cannot praise You
          as You deserve.
Oh, Generous,
You are the healing for my heart.
Oh, Merciful,
How can I know You,
     only You know Yourself.
You are who You say You are
     as You say You are.

Oh, Allah,

You rescue hearts in pain

And bring ecstasy to the hearts of Your
servants.

You illuminate the hearts of Your seekers.

You accept our shortcoming, when confessed.

No one can discover the path towards You
unless You hold one's hand and guide.

Hold my hand and guide me towards the
Real,

There is no one but You who guides.

Give me refuge, protect my heart,
there is no protector but You.

You are the answer to all my prayers

You are the healing for all my pains,

You are the peace that protects me from all
my disturbances.

Oh, Allah,
Whomever searches for You behind the
    covers of reason, adores You out of
    fear or greed.

Whomever loves You for Your kindness,
    will forget You when in sorrow.

Those who seek their own ego as You
    and think fondly that they know You,
    they know You not.

Sufis illuminated by Your light,
    covered by Your rays.
        They are already burning with the
        fire of Your love, and eager to burn
        yet more.

Oh, How I wish that the day comes
When this cage is broken and
    I am called back to my home;

When the way of the people of the world
becomes separated from the way of those
in Union with You;

When the devil hidden behind the face of
the human leaves;

When the Essence of the Kingdom reveals
its Magnificent Face,

And enemy stands apart from Friend.

Hakim Omar Khayam was born in Neyshapour of Khoransan, the northeastern part of Iran, in the middle of the 11th century. Khayam was a philosopher, poet, astronomer, and mystic; his Ruba'iyat are among the most famous works of the world's literature, and have been translated into many languages.

It is said that Khayam was a schoolmate of Khajeh Nezameddin, who became the prime minister of the state, and Hassan Sabah, the great leader of the Ismaili sect, of whom many stories have been told. These three, who grew up together, become outstanding individuals in their own right.

Khayam, who without doubt was a genius, is a universal man. Khayam today is better known for his beautiful and enrapturous poems than for his services to the world of science and astronomy. Thus only a few may be aware that he established the Jallali calendar, a system which was (and still is) among the most accurate astronomical calendars possible using minute calculations to chart how each year changes to the next in an exact computation of hour, minute, and second.

Although Khayam is not commonly considered

to have been a Sufi, the language of his poems strongly suggests that he was at least deeply influenced by Sufism. He was an open minded and free thinking philosopher, and as a result incurred the enmity of the theologians of his time.

The beauty of his words, the intoxicating ideas he presents, and the sensibilities of his heart are not translatable. Who can translate the meaning of love, a meaning to be felt, an art to be understood only in the heart of Khayam. A partial meaning may be understood through the language with which he represents his truths, but in the final analysis the heart of Khayam remains unique in the realm of the centuries that have passed and those that are yet to come.

Khayam speaks of Wine, the extreme love, and God the Wine bearer, who pours the divine Wine into the cup of the heart and takes the drunken *salek*, a spiritual traveler, on an intoxicating voyage. He reminds us that life is passing by where every moment should be celebrated with extreme care.

Hakim Omar Khayam is the master of *ruba'i*, the quatrain, from which the title of his famous work derives. *Ruba'i* usually speak of a philosophical hypothesis or else offer spiritual instruction. The form of *ruba'i* consists of two verses or four half verses forming four lines. This form is tightened still further by a strict meter of which Khayam is the undisputed master. Not only are the endings of the first, second, and fourth lines uniform, but also the letters and the words before the endings have a uniform rhyme. When read out loud, *ruba'i* follows a beautiful melody and can be sung to music.

The sun has thrown the morning
    upon the roof
A king has poured the Wine into the Cup;
"Drink Up!", the Caller at Dawn announced:
    "ashrabu, drink!"
A melody echoed in the cycles of time.

Some say those who stay away from Wine
Live and are born again in human form
    Old friends return as old friends.
I drink Wine and live with the Beloved
If chance permits, we will return together,
    Like old friends.

A vessel of Wine, a book of Love
A loaf of bread to pass the time,
And You and I are in the ruins,
A feast beyond the dream of a king.

O, Sweet Wine Bearer, those past
Rest in the heart of dust.
Listen as you drink your wine:
Every word spoken in truth
    Flies, lost in the wind.

The days of life pass like
Springs of water, and breeze of dawn.
Regret not the day that came not,
Nor the one not yet begun.

Unconsenting I was born
    Into this world of ruins,
Failing in my dreams
    I shall depart to justify the end.
Wine Bearer, rise, bring some Wine
Let us wash away the pain of this
    World with a cup of Wine.

From the heart of the budding rose
    To the star filled heavens
I revealed life's secrets, one after another.
From all secrets I revealed
The death's secret remained hidden
    from my sight.

The heavens whispered a secret to me:
Blame me not for your destiny, fate,
    and life;
If I had the chance or will to change
I would free myself from the
    Whirling of time.

My greed took me to the vessel of Wine
To find the secret of its long life.
It whispered back and said: Drink Wine!
You live and will die, no turning around.

Take a cup of Wine,
    As this is the wealth of the world;
Listen to the harp;
    As it is the psalm of David.
Keep no regret for times come and gone;
Rejoice in life's moments;
    For there is no more to be sought.

Strange! How life's caravan passes
Be wise, rejoice in a moment's peace.
Wine Bearer, shed no tears
   for tomorrow's pain,
For night unfailingly passes into dawn.

The trap of reason will imprison
Those who presume to bargain.
O, you the simple one,
   Choose Wine over all,
Leave those who dry into raisins
   Rather than grow into rich grapes on the vine!

I will take one hundred barrels
   of Wine tonight
Enriching myself in the rounds and
   turnings of the Cups.
I will leave all reason and religion behind
And take the maidenhead of Wine for mine.

I know the reflections of being and
   nothingness;
I know the range of high and low
   Truly, my knowledge surpasses all.
Yet shame upon me if I do not place
Drunkenness higher than all.

Drunken, I passed the Winery the night before
   I saw an aged man, drunk,
      Carrying away yet more Wine.
"You have no shame from the Lord
      Of the World," I said;
"This is the grace of the Lord of the World,"
      He replied.
"Take your cup and let's all become drunken
      And rejoice in the Merciful God."

As a potter fashioned clay into a cup
The clay whispered to him:
      Be kind! my man!
I was not always clay, dust
But was once, like you, a man.

Flee reason and the tangled webs of intellect.
Catch hold of the waves of the Beloved's hair.
Before the destiny of the world
  Takes your life,
Give your life for a Cup of Wine.

Whirlpool of Heavens, our astonishment;
The lamp of our thought, we call its reflection.
Sun is the niche, the universe a lamp
We are the images, wondering in awe.

Khayam, if drunken be happy:
Take the beautiful Beloved and live life.
The world ends in nothing,
So grasp this present moment of Being,
And leave the nothing to naught.

Neither you nor I solved the secret of Being,
Neither you nor I opened the puzzle.
The image of you and I are hidden
    Behind the curtain,
When the curtain falls neither you nor I
    Will remain.

The universe gained nothing from my coming,
Nor will it lose glory from my leaving.
Why did I come and why will I leave?
A secret hidden from all seeing.

Listen to the truth I now reveal:
We are beloved, the world our lover.
Here we are now,
    playing the world's games for a while,
And, then, we depart,
    One by one, into the Nothing

Khajeh Shamseddin Mohammad Hafiz of Shiraz, a 14th century Persian Sufi poet, was born in Shiraz, in central Iran. Shamseddin, his first name, means the sun of religion, while his title, Hafiz, means the memorizer, for he had memorized the Qur'an at a very early age. Hafiz was also called *lesanul gheib*—the language of mystery, the hidden. Hafiz is the master of *ghazal*, the sonnet, love poetry. His book of poetry: Divan has received deserving recognition not only in Iran but also beyond Persian boundaries. For example, Goethe, the German writer of the 18th century, dedicated his collection, *The West-Eastern Divan*, to him.

Hafiz reminds us of the beauty of the Beloved, the Almighty Allah; and the attraction of love: Wine, poured into the Cup of heart by the Merciful Wine Bearer.

Hafiz' mastery is to weave the verses of the Holy Qur'an into poetic imagery, inspiring the lovers of poetry, while revealing the state of the eternal lovers, Sufis. His poems may appear to be simple and smooth, but there is a complex meaning to discover behind each verse.

A field of flowers
A Cup of Wine
And the Beloved by my side,
With such wealth
The king is my servant tonight.
Do not bring in the candle for light
To this gathering tonight:
The Beauty of that Beloved shines
In the house of life.
Wine is not forbidden,
But with Your absence
All is forbidden in my life.
My ears attuned to the music of the reed
And melody of harp;
My eyes search for Your lips,
In the tilting of the Cup.
There is no need for perfume
At this gathering,
The scent of Your hair fulfills my life,
And the sweetness of Your lips
Has no counterpart.
As long as my heart aches for You
A treasure found in the ruins,
I shall dwell close to the ruins of my heart.

Do not blame me for my shame:
My shame is my glory,
There is no grief in my shame.
Do not ask for fame,
There is no blessing in good name.
I am a drunkard ruined and lost,
Like all who dwell here in this town.
Do not complain to the night watchman,
For he is just another drunk.
Hafiz, do not abide without
Wine or the Beloved,
Do not lose the brief life of the flower:
feast and love.
Time is passing, and life is gone.

The end of this place of possibilities
Is not that much!
Offer a cup of Wine,
The world, its rules, its toys
Are not that much!
Honor, life, and heart are
Reflections of the Beloved,
By themselves, life and honor are nothing
much!
Do not beg for shelter,
Nor shade under which to rest,
Know instead that shade or shelter will not
unburden life.
Wealth is the richness of Being;
Be fortunate to gain it all,
In bondage greedy for heaven
Suffer the hardship to arrive
Such heaven and hardship are not that much!
Enjoy the brief life that you are given,
Time will pass, and you will be gone!
Oh, Wine Bearer,
On the shore of annihilation
We are travelers awaiting.
Take a chance in this moment of waiting

The distance between the shore and the ocean
Is not that much!
Oh, Pious ones, you are not safe
From the game of compassion
The distance between the temple
And Winery of Old is not that much!
My pain and my tears,
My everlasting longing,
No need to put them into words!
Such conquest is not that much!
The name of Hafiz is honored
For the people of God,
Whether a good name or disgraced,
The difference is not all that much!

I am a ruin and wisdom's so far away
See the distance between me and the wise.
My heart grows tired of the temples
And the rich robes the deceiver weaves,
Where is the Old Vintage and Pure Wine?
Piety and moral goodness
Have naught to do with ecstasy,
There is not an identity
Between the dry words of a sermon
And the melodies of Divinity.
Blind is the sight of enemies
To the countenance of the Friend,
Fading light is not the same
As pure rays cast by the sun.

Graceful are the memories
Of the day of Unity,
But now she's gone I know not where,
What happened to her coquetry?
Oh friend expect not peace nor patience
Nor restful slumbers from Hafiz.
What now is patience,
Where have rest and
Peace departed to?

Oh, Friends of Allah
I am losing my heart
With pain regretting secrets told.
Mariners on a broken ship
We ask the favored wind to
Waft us forth to see the Friend.
The numbered days of the loving world
Are but dreams of fantasy
Be kind to all, count every blessing.
In a circle ringed with flowers
Sings the nightingale:
I am drunk by dew of Wine.
Salute to You, Maker
Of Miracles—to Your Health!
Come unto me, a worthless drunk.
Hidden in these two bits of counsel
Is the peace of two worlds:
Kindness for friends, for enemies caution.
On the road of good repute
There is no open gate for me;
You look askance, You disapprove
Then make a change in destiny.
The bitterness from You,
Is sweetness for my taste,

Add to my thirst,
Reveal the secrets to me.
Be glad when poor, have mirth, be drunk,
It is the alchemy of being
That transforms poverty to wealth.

Wine Bearer salute the Wise Persians
They are the holders and givers of life.
Oh, forgive me you pious clean-robed Sheikh
This robe of mine is drenched in Wine
Given to me by the Beloved
Hafiz wears it not under his own command.

Oh, Wine Bearer, Come and serve some Wine:
Take us away from the ways of the world
And the sorrows of time past.
Pass me a Cup of Wine
To let me take this dome of heavens and skies,
Condemned both, grace and disgrace:
It matters not what the wise would say.
Free me from hollow vanity,
Curse the hapless ego!
Burning, I lament all these new seekers of love.
I find no one, new or old,
To entrust the safekeeping of my longing heart.
I seek refuge with the Beloved,
Who has robbed me of my peaceful heart.
The beauty of the world grows dim,
The splendor of the forest lessens,
As the beautiful Beloved is unveiled.
Be patient, Hafiz,
In these hard days and nights,
Some day your fortune will come:
Wait until that day arrives.

Last night our Pir left the mosque
For the Winery.
Oh, friends of the path, what should we do?
Where shall we worship or direct our
intention?
Now that our Teacher has sipped the Wine?
In the ruined house of the path,
We dwell side by side:
An Eternal destiny is planned for you and I.
If wisdom were to learn
The joy of heart's submission
To the waves of the Beloved's hair,
The wise would lose their minds in searching
Through the tresses they have lost.
Will the adamantine heart of Yours
Find peace in seeing the burning sighs and
longing of my heart?
The piercing arrow of my lament surpasses
the universe.
Be silent, Hafiz,
Oh, Beloved, have mercy upon Your life
Avoid the arrow of my lament.

Your hair is tangled,
Tossed by the midnight breeze,
Your smile enraptures,
A melody sung, a Cup of Wine.
Your eyes entrancing,
Your lips drunken,
You came to my night
And whispered:
"Oh, the Eternal Lover
Do you sleep tonight?
You are offered the Eternal Wine,
Drink, be drunken remain not an infidel."
Oh, the pious, leave and be gone,
Do not blame the drunkard:
The gift of love is eternal.
I drink what the Beloved offers,
Whether from the springs of the heavens
Or from the Old Vintage.
The laughter of the Wine Bowl,
The tangled hair of the Beloved,
Have broken so many repentant hearts,
Hafiz' is not the only one.

Last night the Beloved came to the
Temple of the Eternal,
All drunken, carrying a bowl of Wine.
We all became besotted,
Looking into her drunken eyes.
The new moon, a mark of her chariot's passing;
Seeing her beauty standing so tall
Even slender Willow went to hide.
How can it be when I am not aware
of my being,
How can it not be when the Beloved is within?
The candle of my being
Expires when she stands high,
Laments that the drunkards
Send up into the heavens,
When she settles into sweet repose.
A fragrance is a
Breeze blown from the scent of her hair.
The black crescent arrow
Found the bow of her brow.
Come back if my passing days
Come back to me
But Pity! An arrow once discharged
Will never fly backwards to its bow.

In these days and times,
A truthful friend is like pure wine, and
The essence of a sonnet, hard to find.
Be cautious, for life's path is narrow,
Now take a cup of Wine
For life is beyond comparing.
I tire of words stripped of deeds:
The vice of the learned who do nothing.
To the eyes of wisdom
This path of distractions,
The world and its destiny, ever changing,
Remain not long.
Caress the hair of the Beloved,
Do not recite the old story,
Of fortune or misfortune,
The signs of Venus or Mars.
My heart hoped to see the beauty of
Your face,
But death remained the highway robber on
the path of life.
I am so drunken with the Wine of Eternity
I'm nowhere to be found
In the revolutions of time.

Love's ocean has no shore to swim for,
The only relief is to give up your life.
The moment of love's rapture
Is the moment of joy;
Waste no time in caution or in doubt.
Bring me a cup of Wine,
Do not bother me with the wisdom of mind
For there is no such guardian in our town.
Ask Yourself, You who sacrifice my life;
My destiny is no reproof to the stars,
Or of the chance of time.
Pure eyes see Your charm,
Not every vision is graced by such warmth.
Honor the moment on this path,
A road that leads to the hidden treasure
Is not open to those who would come with
desire.
I know that my tears could not soften
Your heart,
No matter how I cry out, lamenting,
Your heart remains hard.
No tear can soften Your adamantine heart!

At dawn,
the nightingale called upon the blossom:
Do not tease and torment me so,
There are many blossoms so beautiful
Blooming in this garden of life.
The flower, smiling, whispered back:
True! But no lover is so harsh to the Beloved
as you.
If you long for that cup of jewels
The Old Vintage Wine;
If you wish for the fragrance of love,
Then you must shed many pearly tears
from your eyes.
To breathe the scent of love
One must first kiss
The ground of the Old Winery.
In the garden of heaven
The morning breeze came,
Caressed Hyacinth's tangled hair,
I called upon the throne of seeing:
Where did your eternal vision go?
What a Pity!
The consciousness of riches rest and sleep.

The story of love is not told in words,
So the Wine Bearer offer a cup of Wine,
To bring the talk to its close.
The tears of Hafiz,
Became an ocean to drawn patience and
wisdom
What can I say
The pain of love finds neither rest nor sleep.

A flower field
From the garden of life
Is all I ask.
The presence of the Beloved
From this field of world
Is all I ask.
Forbid the companionship of the hypocrite;
From the heavy load of the world
To abide in this world
Is plenty for me.
Paradise is promised
For the good deed
I am a seeker, a poor man
The Winery of Old
Is all I ask.
Sit by the spring of life
See the passing of days and nights
Of all the signs of the transient
This is enough for me.
What is the world, its promise and its pain
Witnessing such signs
Is enough for me.
Beloved is by my side
No need to ask for anything more,

The riches of her companionship
Is all I ask.
Do not send me to paradise nor to heaven
The riches of being by Your side
Is all I ask.
Hafiz, be fair and blame not destiny
Beauty of your sonnets
Is bountiful enough for those who hear.

The treasure of my chest
Burns with the fire of the heart
In the pain of separation
Fire's in the house,
Consuming my life.
The fever of separation
Deeply burns my body,
The rays of her
Sun-like beauty melts away my life.
A candle came to pity me,
Seeing the tears of my heart,
Becoming like a butterfly it flitted
Circling around my being.
Only such a stranger's heart
Felt my grief as all I lost.
It was a stranger, not a friend
Who thus took pity on my pain.
The robe of my piety
Is drowned in the ruin's waters,
The proud house of my wisdom burnt
By the fire of the vineyards.
I repent
And like a Cup my heart breaks

I become like a tulip's burning heart
Without Wine or Vintage.
Cease the tale, return to me
As I removed the robe
And burnt it as a sign of praise
And thankfulness.
Leave this fantasy, Hafiz,
And drink a little Wine
All awake we spent the night,
And now the candle's melted,
Burnt down to a fantasy.

Oh morning breeze tell me
Where is the Beloved resting?
Where is her dwelling, she who melted
All so many hearts?
In the journey of this dark night
The safe valley lies ahead.
In the Mountain of Tur,
Where is the guiding light,
To announce the Beloved's arrival?
Whoever is born to this world
Has a sign of ruin and loss,
In a ruined world where is wisdom found?
Secret received, secret found
In the world of Secrets
Where can a secret keeper be found?
I long for You
Every bit of my being longs for You,
I am here, annihilated in You
And the useless accuser is busy
With his talks!
You will find my heart lost
Among the tresses
Of the Beloved's waving hair.
Wisdom's mind is lost

Where are the tresses of the beloved's hair?
The heart is lonely hidden in a corner
Where is the beloved's eyebrow?
The Wine Bearer, the melody, and Wine
Have gathered around to feast the time
But, pity! without the Beloved
The joy is lost.
Oh Hafiz, keep yourself from weeping
For the autumn wind that blows
Across the field of life.
Come to your senses and consider,
Is there a single rose without a thorn?

Oh Wine bearer offer some Wine,
Though tranquil was love's first coming,
Now greater hardships love desires.
The misting of pure fragrances
Softly frees her hair at sunrise,
Heart after heart bleeds in longing
For the waves of her black tresses.
Uneasily I linger at the house of the Beloved
Hearing the innkeeper calling,
"Pack up your burdens, soon you'll be going."
Drench your prayer rug with purest Wine
When the Beloved so demands.
Remember that the traveller
Knows the turnings of the path.
Dark is the night, high is the storm,
The twisting pull of the vortex strong,
But those who rest along the shore
With quiet hearts freed from my fears.
I see the fame of my disgrace
Spread to far corners of the world,
For I can no longer conceal
The feast maker of my secrets.
Hafiz, asking for His presence? Do not fall
Into the shadows or dictates of desires.

Gather round, come and rejoicing
Remember that desire's house
Remains not long.
Bring on the Wine
Recalling life's foundation fragile
On the wind.
A dedication to the one who
Under this blue dome of sky
Has freed himself from all the colors
Of this world and its desires.
The secret of the hidden herald
Who brought good tidings when
I was all drunk at the Winery:
Oh you great falcon highest flying
You dwell not here among the ruins.

From highest heavens you are called,
What brings you here to this low place?
Learn and remember, my child,
The same wise counsel that I learned
From the master of my path.
Do not sorrow for the world,
Recall instead what I have learned
Of a passenger of love:

Open your countenance in rest,
Know that the will of destiny
Is hid from the sight of you and I.
Like a bride with many lovers,
World keeps no promises to us.
In the smiling of a flower
There is no pledge of loyalty
Recall the longing song of the nightingale.
Envy not Hafiz's songs,
You who seem so disloyal
For accepting heart
And beauty of my words are gifts from God.

Moulana Shah Maghsoud Sadegh Angha, a twentieth Century Persian Sufi scholar and philosopher, is a master of sonnet and quatrains. There are Sufis who have been regarded as the focal points in the history of Sufism; undoubtedly, in the future, he will be regarded as one of those unique individuals. Moulana Shah Maghsoud has developed a complex language of metaphor and imagery to unveil the mysteries of inner travelling, the heart's longing, and the ultimate destination. Like other distinguished Sufi poets, the verses of the Qur'an and the sayings of the Prophet are woven in his words and metaphors. The metaphor of *Angha* (his pen name) refers to Phoenix, a mythical beautiful bird that burns itself to death to rise from its ashes, and *Ghaf*, to the mountain where *Angha* resides.

Moulana Shah Maghsoud writes in his poems of a heart beating in every particle of the existence that longs for eternal unification, a divine call from the Eternal Beloved is there for those who will listen. Moulana Shah Maghsoud is my physical and spiritual father. In 1980, he has graciously dedicated his *Divan-e-Ghazal*, to me. He begins this magnificent hand written book of poetry, *Divan-e-Ghazal*, with the following *ghazal* (sonnet):

My heart torn in its every beat
By longing for Your love,
Pain of parting drags to dust
My being without cease.
How much longer will You rebel
In communion by the tossing of Your hair?
I beg of You, rebel no more
Against my scattered thought.
Either grasp this heart in Your embracing,
Or brighten with a joyous tulip
The desert that I hold within.
Dream walking guided to Your dwelling,
In the day and by the night,
It matters not to here or there,
Your love leads me where You desire.
With glimmering stars my shirt reflects the
sky,
Those stars are but the diamonds of my tears,
Strewn from the dusk to dawn crying for
Your love,
The beauty of Your face suffices to
Bring ruin to the grounds of piety.
The breeze of dawn upon Your hair
Blows away the faith of all.

The envy of the universe,
You're a coquette, and Your sweetness
Steals many hearts,
Not I alone am captured by Your love.
Angha, the beauty of the sweet Beloved
Robs the heart of my songbird life.

Quatrains:

We searched a while for the Divine
    within the depths of our illusions,
Looking there to find His signs
    in the beings of "You" and "I"
When love appeared
    "You" and "I" were dissolved,
And found no more need
    to follow signs.

Till you stand firm,
    you are not saved.
Until you free yourself and drop
    all signs of self, you are not saved.
You are all when freed
    from self,
But when you are but a tiny cell,
    you are not saved.

Last night, in the gathering of hearts
You were all drunkards,
Finding Your way in my thoughts,
Or was it my dreaming?
You were transformed into
The enfolding hair of the Beloved,
The perfume of the morning breeze,
The drowsy eyes of the lover,
And I found You in all ruins and
    in the corners of love.
You spread your traps, one over another
I am not captured—pick up your traps.
You came arrayed in colors,
But I saw You, the Essence of all.
You marked Your way in the crowd of the
pious,
I saw You drunk,
I found You in the Pure Wine.
You turned into the raindrop,
The ocean, and its thirst,
You became the Winery, the vessel,
The beautiful Wine Bearer,
But I found You in the Cup and the Wine.

Disguise Yourself no longer,
Heart finds no peace in illusion,
I found You, the Sun risen from
The covering clouds.
You turned into One, You turned into All,
Higher, softer, You became wave upon wave,
But I found You in the sea,
And I found You in a mirage, the same.
A cell became human,
A human stepped out from the dust,
A single point gathered all into its being,
And You remained the spirit of the Book.
So many reflections of the beauty
Upon the face of nonexistence,
You called me the falcon of the *Ghaf,*
I saw You searching for the mirror of the
heart.

I thrust aside prayer rug and rosary,
Only love for the Beloved remained.
The sage bears the burden of desire,
And I am eternally drunk
in the circle of love.
Leave behind the common call and prayers,
The deceptive piety of the ignorant,
For only those Divinely guided
Can polish the heart clean of rust.
Seek pain, not its cure,
And come without your ego, and self desire.
If you travel this Path, settle your tent
In the realm of nonexistence, free from it all.
When the drunkard carries the flag
To the roof of the Eternal,
Common knowledge grows like
A thorny vine upon a wall.
In the Winery of the heart
I drink beyond all limit,
My heart made drunk by the eternal Wine.
No robes, no turbans are desired
As I worship in the temple,
As I pray in the Mosque,
I am both drunk and pious

In the Winery and the House of God.
The illuminations of heart form my mirror,
The Tur of all Manifestation within my chest.
I am the secret of Truth
Hidden behind the cycles of being and time.
I am the cloak and the revealer,
I am the Light in the Tur,
The burning bush reflecting that light,
I am Kaaba, the temple, the Gate,
The Cycle within Cycles,
The light of Truth reflected
Upon the tree of life,
Heart becomes the temple of Truth,
I am drunk, reflecting the Divine.
Everyone has taken a path:
Majnun, the lover, took the path of life,
The musician took the path of the reed,
The Wine Bearer, the path of Wine,
And I, Angha, the path with the Beloved,
While Mansur: al Halaj, was drunken
Among the scaffolds of the hanged.

I have broken all my promises to others,
Come to me.
I linger longing in the waves of Your hair,
Come to me.
I dropped the sacred vessel on the ground
And broke the cup of piety,
Come to me.
I tore the beads from the rosary in the temple,
And ripped the prayer beads in the mosque,
Come to me.
No prayer rug, no altar,
I am a simple man, a drunkard, come to me.
I destroyed the trap of deception,
Freed myself from all temptations,
Come to me.
I walk no more, I rest in my pain,
Come to me.
I am a drunkard, wise in the ways of poverty,
I am ruined and enraptured, come to me.

Except for You, Eternal Knower of the Secret,
None knows my world
I am the Angha of the high *Ghaf*
Yet am nothing at Your side.

Quatrain:

I am the treasure hid in ruins
I am the Wine hid in the vineyard's solitude.
Wisdom is limited
    the radiance of my wisdom
Shines cloaked beneath the cover of an
enraptured.

One needs a friend upon the path of love,
An illumination, an intention.
On the way of love, one must become
    the dust
Under the footfalls of the guide,
    A nothing blended with the light of being.

Dance of the Wine!
Bring drunkenness to the eyes!
Watchful wisdom left the road.
The breeze of dawn scatters
Seeing the flower petals of Your hair,
Looking for Your beauty
Heart stopped searching for more.
The drum of ecstasy heard
The melody of Your love,
Followed the rapturous Sufi
To the temple of heart.

Your hair is a veil over the beauty of
Your sunshine,
Did the moon leave the dark night?
Drunkenness turned into piety
Lingering to the curls of Your hair,
Thousands rebelled,
Caused by the waves of Your hair.
Dawn waiting for the sunrise,
Morning rises from the side of the Beloved.
Your being ascends upon the flower petals,
The reflection of the spring fallen upon the
field.

The gaze of the Beloved upon the eastern
Horizon,
Became the ray of the sun,
A spring for Angha's fortune.

Your thought is the companion of my life,
As pain of love dwells as a guest
In the house of heart.
As the veil of night is falling, closing,
The horizon turns into red,
The seal in the tulip's heart,
Blackened by the desert's pain.
Beauty in my words unfolds
Like a bud blossoming reflects Your charm.
Heart is restless;
Its silence is charmed by
Longing for Your love.
I shut my eyes that none may see
The reflection of Your face in my eyes,
The beauty of Your hair,
Reflecting in the mirror,
Waving in Your hair,
Scattering my thoughts.
My bleeding heart resembles not
The laughter of Your red lips, nor does the
Laughter of the flower resemble the long-
waiting bud.
One glance from Your eye,
Shoots an arrow aimed at a thousand hearts,

Every day of Your life
Is a day for the feasting of sacrifice.
No one has seen a grace such as
The bird of Angha,
Whose grace amazes all who ascend
To the skies.

The ocean of love
Is the Wine Bearer and the Winery of heart.
The black seal in the tulip's heart
Is a longing in the field of the heart.
One who seeks the temple of Kaaba
Follows the call of the heart.
The house of reflection has no image,
The shell of the ocean offers the pearl of heart.

Nothing is free from longing for the Beloved,
The two worlds are drunken by the sight of
the heart.
The Messiah's Wine is brewed
And Wine grows old for the longing of heart.

The lover settles in the house of love,
In unity through the steps of the heart
Drawn in the ocean of nonexistence,
The universe drowned in the ocean of the
heart.

I have seen
Your eye as drunken as the Cup of Wine
You lips as warm as the heat radiating
From the Winery.
My heart finds no refuge in pretended love,
Be a butterfly circling closer,
Dare the candle's flame.
Wine Bearer, bring a cup of Wine:
I have seen the beauty of Your eye
In the rounds of Cups of Wine.
The heart is restless,
No need for wisdom to endure
In the story of love.
Every night as I remember Your love,
I see Your infidelity even more.
The secret hidden in Your lips
Is revealed in the Cup and Wine.
You find Your house in the hearts of many,
I have seen hearts ruined by the hand of
Your love.
Angha: the step of intoxication—shatter
Insanity,
A revelation not yet seen,
In fantasy or even in imagination.

No Wine more potent than
The Ruby Wine of the Wine Bearer,
No solitude more peaceful than
The ruined house of the drunkard.
The mark of separation takes the tulip
To the desert,
For patient flowers do not grow
In well-tilled soil of love.
The people of heart take the path of
Annihilation,
Lovers hide not from the sword of hardship.
The flame of life is lit by love
As the heart's fire lights the candle's wick.
The path to the House of the Beloved is
Closed
Except to the rapturous lover.
Watch for illusion, the greatest thief of all
On the path of heart.
The impatient flees from hardship,
But for Majnun, the lover,
Even death is a simple part.
The dawn of knowledge will not bring light
To eyes still sleepy with the night.

The world of Mansur is the world of ego,
An aware heart dares not a claim.
Of the many arrows aimed
At the heart of love,
None is as potent as
The arrow of your sight.
On the way to Kaaba,
Search for the eternal treasure,
The heart of belief not found in
Any rosary or prayer rug.
On the path of love,
Do not claim that you know,
For in the ruins of truth,
No traveler is aware of mind.
The falcon of Angha, sing the eternal song:
Open your ears to
The melodies of the people of heart,
Abounding in secrets.

Hardship! Pity!
If the generous Master does not hold
My hand,
I find no place of refuge,
I desire no helping hand.
Wine Bearer and Eternal Wine
Cannot be found
If the Master of the Eternal does not offer a
Cup.
See here the generosity of the Eternal:
One glance upon my being
And the secret of all Being revealed
To my heart.
The pride of my ego forgotten in
A Cup of Wine,
The kingdom of the world lying at my feet,
And my honor remains in my poverty.
You cannot find the people of the heart
Within the snares of their possessions,
I am the bird of the celestial
Imprisoned in the world of matter.
If you do not desire,
See with the eye of heart
I have no counterpart in the realm

Of ruins of heart.
You were unaware of the Truth
I made you learn,
Now you know, the truth
As I have taught.
I reflect all in the mirror of your heart,
Do not even try to hide,
For I see behind all that is hidden.

Make one curtain drop,
And a thousand veils will fall.
I am the lover, whatsoever You would draw,
You sketch a picture of You, the Beloved.
All are astounded
By my rapture and my dissolution
But my heart and I are in awe
By the magic You put upon us.

Love has no more fear of blame
Than ocean fears a speck of dust,
One who is cured by Jesus' hand
Searches not for pain's releasing.
Dusty stones will not attract
The one who is freed from all clay,
One who drinks from love's own ocean
Will not grow drunk from
A cup or a drop of wine.
Throw not the beauty of Your tresses
Entwining there to capture me,
For I
Fall willing into Your love's embraces.
Keep silent, my heart,

Are your senses lost
Amidst too insane a drunkenness?
Put aside the cup and take the bowl,
To rise with rapture as you drink the Wine
And sit to music dancing to its strains.
Last night I knocked on every door
Asking for a cup of Wine.
All doors were closed except
Heart's own door,
As I entered its house I stood and heard:
You've searched in vain before false doors.
The wings of heart that flying,
Searching, falling into
Many snares,
Cannot brag of the *Ghaf* and wing of Angha.

Do you know me, oh dear heart?
I am but life from the Beloved.
Not just mere clay but rather
The light of the heart
Breathed into the heart of dust.
I am the soul of the spirit,
My heart resides beyond the spheres.
My life springs forth from His commanding,
Earth from heaven, life hid in dust.
I fall like the crying rain
Upon the smiling flower,
As I remain upon this globe
In smiles and in tears.
Divine willed and said:
"I am!
I am Life, I am all."
Gaze forth at destiny and see
How life is hid in body.
Pure mirror of my heart's reflecting
Divine light,
In every breath
Truth's image cast onto my being
Every moment of life.

The hidden guide of truthfulness
Accompanied me on a safe journey
From dark *nafs* to life's waters searching.
Searching for Truth
A quest eternal and deserving,
Like nonexistence I appear concealed
Apparent and hidden
From eternal to eternity.
Guarded by Divine, it is not my way
That takes me past my limitations.
I have seen the light of
The Friends of the Divine
From the depths of the:
"Hidden treasure."
If you long for pain,
My guide knows its healing.
In the pure face of Mohammad
I have seen the light of Ali,
All that exists astounded by my secrets.
I am the falcon of the Master,
I am the Angha of the dear *Ghaf*
Enraptured and drunken am I
Singing my songs.

Majnun's tale and mine are not the same,
For no two pains exist alike
In this universe's broad expanse.
Destiny's lash breaks not my heart,
Nor do the passing shadows of the waves
Remain engraved upon the sea.
The pebbles cast by life's events
Shattered my cup
Purity remains not with the crystal ball.
Your eye's glance reflects a world to me,
For without Your sight my steps would falter.
The storm raised by Your disloyalty
Does not surpass my heart's journey
For Your love.
Two worlds are searching to buy my heart,
Why does Your pain not honor that heart?
Forever supreme is Your beauty in rapturous
Kaaba.
No one would dare compete with such
beauty.

When the bride of Your beauty enters the
garden

Heaven's beauty will hide and fade away.

Your love is my heart's teacher,
Your praise cannot be fully written.
I am my own lord seeking no one's help,
A flower seeks no shade from weeds.
Angha does not take like falcon
Know that myth is no lesser than truth.

I am that reed knowing not its song,
I am a parrot needing no reward.
Yeah and Nay spring but from Being,
Reflections of eternal love,
In itself the *la*'s negations
Is the affirmation of *ela*'s.
If the raindrop knew its fate,
And could see the vastness of the ocean,
It would not remain an empty
Bubble caught between two worlds.
Remain alive within the Divine,
Release your self the images of "we" and "I,"
For in dying is the breaking
From the figures of all.
The bloom of life needs the craft of a guide
To rise free from the images of illusion.
Those ruined, drunk with the Eternal Wine,
Are drunken to the end
For their eternal unity.
These Sufis drink the vintage of unity,
Released from duality
By the means of their own unity.
What is that rosary, which,
Annihilated, the Sufi has fastened?

It is the sign of life's servitude fastening
He, who is the master of his own.

Ego is a wasteland ruining a seed
How long can one serve such a fruitless
destiny?
Is the *Ghaf* of Angha the center of being,
As it is hidden while apparent in every cell?

How many times did I remind you, heart,
Not to cherish hope of these people,
To remain instead alone and raptured,
Mixing only with Wine and drunkenness?
Only in silent listening to the words
Of the masters of the meaning
May you learn the truth.
Why do you run from me in haste?
As if I were drunken and you sober?
Just a few more days of loyal patience I ask.
The worldly Sheikh will not discover
Drunkenness within the Wine,
Even should he forever carry
His haughty robe of piety.
If the crowds of ignorant praise you,
Recall that to the drunken ones
Wisdom has no value.
There is no rejoicing and no rapture
In the singing of the wise,
But it is the drunkard who may tear
The curtain of drunkenness when he hears,
"Salute!"
If a breeze brings a message

From the dwelling of the Friend,
Life can be given as the reward
To the bearer of the message.
Make an ocean of your heart,
Break the shore in every wave
With every step you take.
An ocean,
Not a spring busy with
The road and pebbles, waves, and shore.

Every time I sip the Wine,
I take it from the Beloved's hand.
So I receive and drink,
And so with Wine grow drunk.
From that Wine seller I have learned
The ways of drinking:
Prepare for such a feast and drink when
ready.
If I should live I'll sacrifice
My life at the feet of the Wine Bearer,
If fortune remains,
I'll hold the Beloved in my arms.
As I made wisdom busy with
The changing lines of the shore,
I reach to pull out of the depths
Of this great ocean of insanity
The pure gem.
Her black hair binds my heart's feet
See my submission to an infidel's snare!
The sun's radiance in her face is in
The heart of every particle,
And I am like a wave
Glimpsing into every cell.
Through her parting elixir of alchemy

My face becomes golden,
And so I could plunge the heart
Of the universe into red fire.
I am the songbird of the Divine,
And in the depth of richness,
Should I destroy this cage
I shall fly from this bowl of dust.

Quatrain:

Alas, the beautiful Beloved did not live long,
Alas, that enchanting Wine Bearer departed,
And the cup did not endure.
Such is the disloyalty of that Beauty,
Like the bloom upon a flower,
Borne on the branch of life at dawn,
That did not last and died by night.

Ezzeddin Nasafi was one of the Sufi scholars of thirteenth century, Persia, whose book: *Insan-e-Kamel*, has been considered as one of the major texts for Sufi studies. This book consists of twenty two treatises and each treatise contains chapters dedicated to Sufism and its principles, addressing the state of the Perfect Human, in the context of Sufism. The followings are teachings from this book:

Oh, my friend:
Love makes the world of creation a possibility and the ecstasy of ascension a will.
Look around yourself and see a universe saturated by the fragrance of love.

If there was no love and the endurance for such longing, then who could beautify words into majestic melodies?

If there was no breeze to gracefully caress the hair of the beloved, then how could the lover see the revealing face of the beloved?
Such longing is to gracefully return to the Provider, in the state of perfection.

Oh, my friend:
do not become slave of worship, but
understand the meaning of worship;
understand the meaning of Divine, Allah,
and practice to be pious and peaceful;
become a true human being, as becoming a
true human being is the key to salvation.

Oh, my friend:
if you have chosen an inner path, remember
that we all are travelers, our moments are
passing and we are passing with them.

Your wealth will not remain forever and your
pain will not last, so do not become a slave to
your wealth nor to your pain.

If you are a person of an inner path, then you
are a person of peace, so make peace with
yourself and your surroundings.